The Gift
of
Who I AM

Living Prayer Series: Book 1

Gifted to & Shared by

Christine Black Cummings
Illustrated by Diane McClary

Balboa Press books may be ordered through booksellers or by contacting:

Balboa Press
A Division of Hay House
1663 Liberty Drive
Bloomington, IN 47403
www.balboapress.com
844-682-1282

ISBN: 978-1-9822-5932-7 (sc)
ISBN: 978-1-9822-5933-4 (e)

Print information available on the last page.

Balboa Press rev. date: 05/12/2022

BALBOA.PRESS
A DIVISION OF HAY HOUSE

And so "The Gift" came…

On a solitary walk at The Living Desert, Palm Desert, CA, in April 2013, *The Gift* began gifting itself to me. Thanks to Julia Cameron's *The Artist's Way* and the teachings of Ernest Holmes *Science of Mind,* I knew to listen. And to transcribe its words. Shortly thereafter, I shared what I thought was a complete poem of 140 words in seven stanzas of four lines each with encouraging classmates at The Center for Spiritual Living. I added the rainbow I'd photographed in Hawaii the previous month, created bookmarks and gave them as gifts.

Likely due to my receptivity immediately after I sent to my publisher the manuscript of the book I'd been writing for 12 years, *Black-Eyed Susan - A Love-Child Finds Her Father and Her Self, The Gift* kept giving and growing, reaching pretty much its current form in December of that year.

Although I had clarity that The Great Creator had delivered *The Gift* to me, I kept asking, "What is it?" And, "Why me?" Because it sounded like poetry from my childhood and I felt no urge to make edits, I came to believe its message was one my angry 13-year-old self opted to ignore when I decided I didn't need a father—heavenly or earthly—in my life. This time, 67-year-old me listened, absorbed and, as instructed in *The Gift*, "Put me in your pocket and hold me in your heart."

My heart kept reminding me that *The Gift* wasn't ***just*** for me. So I asked, "What am I to do with it?" The answer I kept hearing was, "Share." And so I shared, from time to time, with selected friends and family. At an altar of creativity in an *Artist's Way* creative circle, I rolled it out as 12 parchment paper scrolls, was awed and motivated by the response I received, especially from Rev. Dale Olansky.

I have come to believe that each of us—you, me, all humanity—is a "God Gift" to the world. We are all uniquely gifted by The Giver of All that IS—the ultimate, everlasting I AM. It is my prayer that this ***Living Prayer*** inspires you and others to show up in life as "The Gift" YOU are created to be. May you be bountifully blessed as you share ***The Gift of Who YOU Are*** and your unique gifts in ways that help create a world that works for the highest and best of all.

Honoring the Legacy of Tyler Cummings

The *Gift of Who I AM* is dedicated to and honors our grandson Tyler Curtis Cummings and how he showed up in the world. *The Gift's* words were gifted to me in 2013 during the time Tyler was undergoing tests to determine the cause and prescribe treatment for what turned out to be a rare neurological disorder. My heart feels its CONNECTion to Tyler. At Tyler's Celebration of Life in July of 2019, family, friends, classmates, teachers and others spoke of Tyler's brave, loving, giving, caring, sharing legacy that continues to inspire them.

May Tyler's legacy touch your heart in a rainbow of uplifting ways.

This rainbow appeared over Black Rock, CT, Harbor on 7-17-2019, Tyler's first full day in *The Next Place.* I believe Tyler continues to smile at us via rainbows, angel clouds and many more ways that his sweet soul reminds us of *The Gift* he continues to be.

Celebrating Casey Cummings

Just as Tyler held his sister Casey's hand walking with her to kindergraden, Casey was with Tyler - as his best buddy - throughout every step of his earthly journey. Their forever connection continues as Casey processes the grief of losing her best friend and shares her writing about grieving to help others whose loved ones are no longer with them physically. As President of Best Buddies at Joel Barlow High School, Casey advocates for special needs students to be included in the lives of all students. Congratulations, Casey, for winning Scholastic's Silver Award for *On Grieving,* which I gratefully share on Pages 26 & 27.

Gratitude for Tyler's Circle of Love and Care

Steve, Kelly and Casey Cummings
Aunt Wendy, Uncle Jeff, and cousins Cooper and Kensey Diglio
Dr. Thomas Homa, Dr. Amy Weinrib and the loving staff at Pediatric Healthcare Associates,
Boston Children's Hospital, National Institute of Health
Joel Barlow High School, Easton/Redding, CT, The Black Rock Community, Bridgeport, CT
Double H Ranch, WWE, Make-A-Wish,
Regional Hospice, Danbury, CT for being the perfect place for Tyler and his loved ones, with
special thanks to Jennifer Matlack and others who cared for Tyler and who support Casey.
Family, friends and others from so many places. To each, thank you.

My Personal Gratitudes

To all who have inspired me, and to you and others
who have accompanied me on my spiritual journey, thank you.
To others who love and support me in so many other ways
—especially you, my beloved Dave—
I gratefully appreciate each of you.
To my believers and encouragers with whom I shared *The Gift of Who I AM*,
my grateful heart overflows to each of you. To the Spiritual Center of the Desert, Palm
Desert, CA, especially Rev. Dale Olansky and Dr. Laura Shackelford whose enthusiasm
and prayers propelled me to take action on sharing *The Gift of Who I AM:*
I appreciate the Light you shine and for being my spiritual home.
Thank you, Dr. James Mellon, our Spiritual Leader, for uplifting me and others to
"Love Only - Forgive Everything - Remember Who You Are" and **"Do It Now!"**
And to know: **"Wherever I Am, God Is."**
For daily email inspiration from Dr. Maxine Kaye, Alan Cohen, Neale Donald Walsch,
Rev. Christian Sorensen, Unity's *Daily Word* and Sarah Young's *Jesus Calling,*
plus Karen Drucker, Daniel Nahmod, Karl Anthony and other spiritual singers and empowering
retreat/workshop/"play shop" leaders: in Karen's words: *I am so grateful, I am so blessed.*
I appreciate all in Unity's *Daily Word* 7 AM Meditation Circle I lead at Chaparral
Country Club for their sharing, caring, prayers, love and laughter.
Mary Ellen Peterson, thank you for the colorful prayer shawl that graces this book.
And for my amazing 8 AM Prayer Partner Suzanne Stradley, gratitude abounds.
Thank you Mom (Mor-Mor to many) for teaching me that getting up early is a gift.
You are a gift whose life and legacy continue to inspire.

And to YOU who are reading this, I am grateful for you.

Diane McClary, a gifted *plein air* painter, has honed her skills studying under master teachers and shared her gifts as artist and painting teacher for over four decades. Diane's jewel-like oil paintings are alive with her attention to light and color, reflecting her innate understanding that less is very often more. Diane's persona reflects the excitement and joy that painting brings to her life.

Two years ago, Diane and her husband Dan sold their La Quinta, CA, home and moved to Chaparral Country Club in Palm Desert. Shortly thereafter, Diane walked into the 7 AM *Daily Word* Meditation Circle I lead. Since then, Diane's radiant positivity, faith, resilience and generosity have added so much to our gatherings and to my life, most recently when she gifted me with the use of her glorious paintings to illustrate *The Gift of Who I Am*. I am so grateful that I am so blessed.

Connect with Diane and view more of her artistry on her website: DianeMcClary.com. Email her at mcclarydi@aol.com. Her artwork is also available at www.Fineartamerica.com.

Table of Contents

The Gift

I live in sparkling waters,
In every grain of sand.
I live on snow-capped mountains
And in the heart of man.

I live in far off cities,
In nearby hamlets too.
I am the sacred Spirit
That lives and breathes as you.

I smile at your successes,
I cry when you're in pain.
I cleanse you from all ailments,
Like gently falling rain.

I am your close companion,
In every breath you take,
The light that always guides you,
Not ever to forsake.

Of all your earthly presents,
I am the best by far,
The source of all your knowing,
Your brightly shining star.

So put me in your pocket,
And hold me in your heart.
Know we are together,
Never to be apart.

I am with you always,
Through endless shades of time,
Dimensions beyond knowing,
Forever intertwined.

The Promise

I live in all my children,
Waiting to reveal
The greatest of all mysteries,
The innate power to heal.

I keep my rainbow promise
To always be your friend,
Your confidante, companion,
A love that never ends.

In waters calm and choppy,
In turbulence and swells,
I am the anchor always
The truth that all is well.

Accept from me the bounty,
See full the cup of life.
Savor every blessing
No need to live in strife.

Delight in what confounds you,
Elusive though it be.
I promise all the answers
When you rely on me.

Store me in your heartbeat,
To quicken every step.
Allow my hand to guide you
And help you stand erect.

So listen closely always,
And patiently await
Your resurrected greatness
Ready to partake.

The Power

I am the power within you
That meets your every need,
The garden that will flourish
As you nurture precious seeds

I meet you in the sunshine
Of each beloved face.
I hold your hand and whisper,
"I am amazing grace."

Cherish quiet moments,
Embrace your soul divine.
Be open when I prompt you
With what I have in mind.

I'm ready when you call me,
Our partnership ordained.
I am the voice that whispers,
"Together, yes, we can."

I'm with you when you wander,
Or fail to take a stand.
I redirect your footsteps;
I am your promised land.

I give to you the courage
That as you take my way,
The gift of new beginnings
Turns darkness into day.

Savor the joy of living
The recreated you,
The gift that keeps on giving,
A love forever true.

The Message

I am a new day dawning
The bell that ceaseless tells
A harbinger of goodness
Reflecting all is well.

Live fully in the moment,
Let no worry cloud today.
With open heart and gratitude,
Acceptance is the way.

Listen for my promptings
Drink deep the well of truth
In quiet contemplation,
Tap your deepest root.

Hear me in words of sages,
In prince and pauper too.
They bring my one great message,
Customized for you.

Accept surprising packages
That come from near and far
May bear a gift of Spirit:
"I love you as you are."

Resist the urge to label;
All can help you learn.
Give thanks for what is given;
Old bridges learn to burn.

If messengers confuse you,
First settle into me.
I offer up the answer,
The truth that sets you free.

The Comfort

If busyness bewilders
Or troubling times you face,
Seek first my inner guidance,
In silence breathe my grace.

My arms are here to comfort,
My hands to guide your way.
Just enter into silence
And hear what I will say.

If ever you feel lonely
Know I am at your side.
Embedded in your heartbeat,
Your ever, inner guide.

Find me in grassy meadows,
Sink into new-mown grass.
I'm there to reassure you
Of what is sure to pass.

Step into like a child
The garden of your grace.
In innocence surrender
And let me light your days.

Seek solitude and savor
The food that feeds you best;
Your inner craving satisfied
When in me you find rest.

I am the nightbird calling
The ending of each day.
I promise new beginnings
As troubles pass away.

10

Diane McClary

The Commission

Tell all my precious children
The truth of who they are.
Remind them of their greatness,
The glow that is their star.

Embrace your brother always,
Know differences you share
Are butterfly reminders
Of diversity so rare.

N'er exclude another,
Instead connect as one.
Pray with great abandon,
Give thanks that it is done.

Come out from every closet,
My great glad tidings tell,
A symphony of sameness,
The you I know so well.

Challenge not your neighbor,
Nor differences offend;
Follow my example,
Love each one as a friend.

Celebrate in Oneness
Of fellowship divine.
Reach out in tender mercy
To hands that all hold mine.

Regardless of behavior,
Treat each one as a friend,
Your sanctified commission
To live the love I am.

The Garden

Plant seeds of kindness always
And nurture them with love.
Gardens bloom and flourish
In sunshine from above.

Harvest from my bounty,
I am the bread of life.
My nourishment sustaining
In joy as well as strife.

Honor all my flowers,
So colorful, so rare;
A living testimonial
To tender, loving care.

Savor the holy essence
Its fragrance bold and sweet.
My energy then radiate
To all you see and greet.

Reach out in compassion
To those who are in need.
A smile or a handshake
May grow a ready seed.

Share my simple pleasures,
A ray of golden sun,
A wink, a hug, a whisper,
Confirm that all are one.

Like daffodils that linger
As sunny memories,
My radiance, my brilliance
Lighten all your needs.

14

The Possibility

Anchor not to sameness,
Newness is my way,
Welcome possibilities
In tides that harbor change.

If caught in stormy weather,
Navigate by faith.
Agree to let me lead you,
To places you'll be safe.

Seek holy sanctuary
In fellowship divine.
Our mystic sweet communion
Is all you need to find.

Consider new prescriptions,
In me you're to abide,
Your resident physician,
Forever at your side.

Be confident, courageous,
Let mercy be your guide,
Reap from my abundance
For you I will provide.

Iron out the wrinkles,
Stitch each undone seam.
Don garments of perfection,
The ones I choose to see.

Surrender to life's changes,
To those of every kind.
Together work the power,
And untold glories find.

16   Diana McClary

The Trust

Trust that I sustain you
In times both bad and good.
In unity is wholeness
In peace is brotherhood.

If darkness holds you captive,
See your hand holding mine.
My light will always guide you
To what you need to find.

Believe life is eternal,
Prepare to claim the prize
The mystery unfolding
For all who realize.

Though days on earth are numbered,
Fear not what you face.
Nestle into trusting
The last hurrah is grace.

My light shines on forever,
Its penetrating rays
Promise each beginning
Is near, not far away.

Keep in concert always
With those whose days are done,
A prelude to my mystery
The loud amen of one.

My Spirit fills you always
In this life and beyond,
A light that glows eternal
A joy that knows no bounds.

The Work

You're here as a reminder
Through endless sands of time,
My passionate expression,
The one I claim as mine.

Like diamonds on the water
Clear and sparkling true,
A beautiful unfolding
The gift I made as you.

Embrace your sacred service
Give because you care;
Your time, passion, talent,
My gifts for you to share.

Act like you're a winner,
Step out and play the game
Teammates and opponents
In my eyes are the same.

Put your best foot forward,
Unite with me and see,
The rarified expression
I mean for you to be.

Let passion inspire your action,
Use me to provide
The fuel for every journey,
Including one inside.

Tell all I am the answer
They have been searching for.
Just listen closely always
To what I have in store.

The Way

I speak to you in nature
In its diverse array,
As much when sleet or fog-bound
As on a sun-kissed day.

The gentle joy of birdsong
The calming hum of grass
Like angel wings uplifting
From what has come to pass.

Though winds of change may threaten
The status quo you know;
I'm here to help you weather
Whatever life bestows.

So harken to all voices
Not only ones you know;
See me in muddy water
As well as pure white snow.

Glee can live in puddles,
So step right in and see
The joy of new adventures
The possibilities.

Bequeath to gentle giants
The kindness they exude;
When you take off the blinders
My sight all clouds remove.

Stand tall and grounded always
To weather any storm;
I am the one safe passage
That keeps you from all harm.

22

The Light

I live in Mother Mary
As baby Jesus too,
In Joseph and the innkeeper
My light shines brightly through.

I live in wise men following
The star that lights their way,
In shepherds looking out for
All sheep that go astray.

A baby in a manger,
I am the prince of peace,
Your transport to the heartland
Where pain and trouble cease.

A love that never changes
A ray of golden light
Full orbed in all its glory
An incandescent sight.

I am the new day promise
I am the risen son
The perfect orchestration
When time on earth is done.

I live as multiplicity
The gift each person brings.
Salute the best in all you meet,
Regard each as a king.

I live as your uniqueness,
The gift of who you are.
Unwrap your hidden gemstones,
Go shine your light afar.

My Personal Reflections

As you reflect on *The Gift of Who I AM,* ask yourself: When **something greater** speaks, am I listening?
As I listen, do I hear? As I hear, am I open to receive?
As I receive, do I use the gifts I receive in ways that benefit and prosper me and others too?

This page is for **your** Personal Reflections

_____

_____

_____

_____

_____

_____

_____

_____

_____

_____

_____

_____

_____

_____

_____

_____

My Living Prayers

My prayer is that this ***Living Prayer*** helps you find new ways
to live with ease and grace and to live and give more joyfully and generously.

This page is for **your** Living Prayers for yourself, others and our world.

_____
_____
_____
_____
_____
_____
_____
_____
_____
_____
_____
_____
_____
_____
_____
_____
_____

On Grieving

By Casey Cummings

There is no way to describe grief in a simple sentence that would be easy enough for a kid to understand, and there is no way to put it that would give someone an understanding of what it feels like, and there is no way to prepare for it. It hurts, it's unforgiving, it's exhausting, it's numbing, it's tirelessly and hopelessly too much.

The grieving process is not the straight line some people hope it is going to be. When death comes, you are numb for a while, people bring you breakfast and cry with you in your living room, candles are lit, and the services are a blur. You go through the five stages, you learn to heal, and then you're all done. If I am being honest, the five stages of grief are a load of crap. Denial. Anger. Bargaining. Depression. Acceptance. That is the order that the online searches of desperation give you, and that is all they give. What Google doesn't tell you is that someday you are going to be angry and the next day you feel like you have come to some sort of peace, and then the next day you hurt so badly that a promised smoothie couldn't even get you out of bed. There is no timeline, there is no direct process, and there is no way someone could tell you how to do it.

There are things that help, don't get me wrong. Coping strategies are honestly the best aid you are going to find when grieving. Some people write, that's what I do. Some people turn to their faith and some people turn to a therapist. Fidget toys and happiness in a pill. Drowning yourself in work, food, substance abuse, anything you can get your hands on. Coping methods are hit or miss. You try one and turn to another when the first attempt doesn't work. That is just how it is, one try and you move on. It isn't that you want to give up. The weight that you feel on your chest and shoulders and legs and heart is just too heavy to wait around and give something another try. You learn to decide what is worth keeping around and what makes things harder to heal. Sometimes you have to shut out people and sometimes you have to shut out every single thing that reminds you of what has been lost. Triggers and reminders give you chills or scary thoughts or sadness or relief. Every day of grief is different. It is a rollercoaster with thousands of loops within each other.

The most irritating part of grief is how people try to understand and help when they've never gone through anything similar. "I am so sorry, you are so strong," or "I know he is watching over you," or "Don't have regrets." To someone grieving, hearing these things feels like a punch to the gut. The intentions are kind, but it is the reactiveness rather than proactiveness that doesn't give any sense of ease. All grievers know their strength. Getting out of bed each day is enough in itself. Our world fell apart while others watched and moved on. That hurts more than anyone could ever imagine, and we can't do anything about it because that is not ours to control. Focus, hope, and happiness are crippled so deeply that every emotion death brings takes over. It is a sad reality, truly. Besides your family, no one will understand what has actually happened. And even within your own family there are going to be differences. A 16-year-old sister who is now an only child and just trying to find her way through high school while maintaining her grades and losing friends and forming her future. A mom who lost her firstborn child, who put her all into his care and fights every day to make sure her daughter is getting by, putting her before everything. A father who lost his best friend and can't even explain how he is feeling. Grief is scary and strange and everything in between. No one knows how to deal with it, and everyone turns to different things. There is no process, no matter who tells you that and what you read online.

I don't know how one could put grief into words and I don't think one will ever learn. It is a weight that you now carry and will never find the destination to drop it off. Grief is never paradise; it is a whole lot of pain. But the pain you feel is because of the love that is there and lives forever. Death might take away who you love, however you will never stop loving them. But how is love redefined now that it coexists with grief? Do you love them just the same, or even more? To the world, that emotion is only present when you do things that your person loves. On their birthdays and holidays, you feel love and know they are with you. "They are loving you from heaven!" Well maybe. But who decided that you had the power to say that? No one has the power to speak for your emotions and your loved ones' emotions because we just don't know. But what we do know is that we actually hate doing the things that we saw they did every day. We hate birthdays and holidays; we have no reason to celebrate. You claim that they love us from heaven, but they aren't even here to show it. There are no hugs, no comfort, nothing that even points to us getting love. But it synchronizes with grief because it is there, just in a different way. Love is there through the joy when we finally accomplish something. Love is there when you follow your dreams, and you know your brother is proud. Love is there when you are holding your mom so tight that her sobs become earth-shattering, but you are crying with her. The togetherness. Love is there when you reminisce with your dad about the April Fools prank you played on him, a glass of water with a surprise. You feel their love within you, not when you do things that they loved. It's not around you, but it is a part of your heartbreak. It is within each bond of the hydrogen and oxygen that make up your oh so present tears. It is the bass of your screams and the transitions of your words. And that is what a kid should learn about grief.

Grief is a whole lot of love.

Printed in the United States
by Baker & Taylor Publisher Services